W9-APM-676

FREDERICK COUNTY PUBLIC LIBRARIES

Readers' Theater: How to Put on a Production

Ghosts and Gummy Worms

A Readers' Theater Script and Guide

Looking Glass Library

An Imprint of Magic Wagon
abdopublishing.com

By Nancy K. Wallace   Illustrated by Lucy Fleming

To all my theater kids at the library! —NKW
To Dawn and Jonathan. —LF

abdopublishing.com

Published by Magic Wagon, a division of ABDO, PO Box 398166, Minneapolis, Minnesota 55439.
Copyright © 2016 by Abdo Consulting Group, Inc. International copyrights reserved in all countries. No
part of this book may be reproduced in any form without written permission from the publisher.
Looking Glass Library™ is a trademark and logo of Magic Wagon.

Printed in the United States of America, North Mankato, Minnesota.
042015
092015

THIS BOOK CONTAINS
RECYCLED MATERIALS

Written by Nancy K. Wallace
Illustrations by Lucy Fleming
Edited by Heidi M.D. Elston, Megan M. Gunderson & Bridget O'Brien
Designed by Laura Mitchell

Library of Congress Cataloging-in-Publication Data

Wallace, Nancy K.
  Ghosts and gummy worms : a readers' theater script and guide / by Nancy K. Wallace ; illustrated by Lucy
Fleming.
     pages cm. -- (Readers' theater: how to put on a production set 2)
  ISBN 978-1-62402-113-8
1. Halloween--Juvenile drama. 2. Theater--Production and direction--Juvenile literature. 3. Readers' theater--
Juvenile literature. I. Fleming, Lucy, illustrator. II. Title.
  PS3623.A4436H35 2015
  812'.6--dc23
                              2015001639

Table of Contents

Celebrate with a Play!

Everyone loves holidays! Some schools and libraries hold programs or assemblies to commemorate special occasions. This series offers fun plays to help celebrate six different holidays at your school or library. You can even sell tickets and use your play as a fund-raiser.

Readers' theater can be done very simply. The performers sit on stools or chairs onstage. They don't have to memorize their lines. They just read them.

Adapted readers' theater looks more like a regular play. The stage includes scenery and props. The performers wear makeup and costumes. They move around to show the action. But, they still carry their scripts.

Readers' theater scripts can also be used for puppet shows. The performers stand behind a curtain, move the puppets, and read their scripts.

Find a place large enough to put on a play. An auditorium with a stage is ideal. A classroom will work, too. Choose a date and ask permission to use the space. Advertise your play with posters and flyers. Place them around your school and community. Tell your friends and family. Everyone enjoys watching a fun performance!

Tickets and Playbills

Tickets and playbills can be handwritten or designed on a computer. Be sure tickets include the title of the play. They should list the date, time, and location of the performance.

A playbill is a printed program. The front of a playbill has the title of the play, the date, and the time. The cast and crew are listed inside. Be sure to have enough playbills for the audience and cast. Pass them out at the door as the audience enters.

The Crew

Next, a crew is needed. The show can't go on without these important people! Some jobs can be combined for a small show.

Director — organizes everyone and everything in the show.

Costume Designer — designs and borrows or makes all the costumes.

Stage Manager — makes sure everything runs smoothly.

Lighting Designer — runs spotlights and other lighting.

Set Designer — plans and makes scenery.

Prop Manager — finds, makes, and keeps track of props.

Special Effects Crew — takes care of sound and other special effects.

Sets

At a readers' theater production, the performers can sit on stools at the front of the room. An adapted readers' theater production or full play will require sets and props. A set is the background that creates the setting for each scene. A prop is an item the actors use onstage.

Scene 1 will need a paintbrush and paint can for when Will pretends to paint the pumpkin. He also needs a rag to clean off the brush.

Scene 2 takes place outside the school. You can make trees with bare branches out of cardboard or cut some real branches and put them in small buckets or cans full of sand. Paint a mansion on cardboard to have toward the back of the stage. Scatter fake leaves on the floor.

Scene 3 and **scene 5** can be performed with or without backdrops. If you use a backdrop, paint cardboard to look like a wall in a house or cover the cardboard with wallpaper. Use different wallpaper on each side so it can be used for the two different houses.

Scene 4 will use the same mansion from scene 2. Caution tape can be up against the house or set up to look like it's blocking off a sidewalk area.

Props

- Several pumpkins
- Paintbrush
- Paint can
- Rag

- Bowls
- Snacks
- Cupcakes
- Cookies

- Bottles of water
- Flashlights
- Trick-or-treating bags
- Mugs

The Cast

Decide who will play each part. Each person in the cast will need a script. All of the performers should practice their lines. Reading lines aloud over and over will help the performers learn them. *Ghosts and Gummy Worms* needs the following cast:

James — Alex's older brother

Alex — James's younger brother

Will — James's best friend

Emma — a friend and classmate

Kyrsten — a friend and classmate

Miss Craig — a new teacher

Makeup and Costumes

Makeup artists have a big job! Every cast member wears makeup. And, stage makeup needs to be brighter and heavier than regular makeup. Buy several basic shades of mascara, foundation, blush, and lipstick. Apply with a new cotton ball or swab for each cast member to avoid spreading germs.

Costume designers set the scene just as much as set designers. They borrow costumes or adapt old clothing for each character. Ask adults for help finding and sewing costumes.

Most of the time, the performers can wear regular clothes they would wear to school. The later scenes are the exception.

James, **Alex**, **Will**, Emma, **Kyrsten**, and **Miss Craig** will all need Halloween costumes.

Rehearsals and Stage Directions

After you decide to put on a play, it is important to set up a rehearsal schedule. Choose a time everyone can attend, such as after school or on weekends. Try to have at least five rehearsals before the performance.

Everyone should practice together as a team, even though individual actors will be reading their own scripts. This will help the play sound like a conversation, instead of separate lines. Onstage, actors should act like their characters even when they aren't speaking.

In the script, stage directions are in parentheses. They are given from the performer's point of view, not the audience's. Actors face the audience when performing, so left is on their left and right is on their right.

Some theater terms may be unfamiliar:

Curtains — the main curtain at the front of the stage.

House — the area in which the audience sits.

Wings — the part of the stage on either side that the audience can't see.

Right Wing
Stage Right

Upstage
Center Stage
Downstage

Left Wing
Stage Left

Script: Ghosts and Gummy Worms
Scene 1: The Auditorium

(Will is painting a giant pumpkin. James walks on from stage right.)

James: Hey, nice pumpkin! I *love* Halloween!

Will: Yeah, me too. I especially love all that candy.

James: I like the spooky stories. Someday, I hope I'll see a real ghost.

Will: Not me, man. I'll pass. I don't like being scared to death.

James: Is that pumpkin for the school play?

Will: Yes, Miss Craig asked me to paint some of the props and scenery.

James: She seems super nice! Last week, she brought kites for everyone in Alex's class. They flew them up on the hill behind the school for science class.

Will: Wow, science wasn't like that when I was in second grade!

James: I know, right? And Alex says Miss Craig never yells at her class!

Will: I wish we were that lucky. She's the first new teacher we've had in town in years!

James: I heard she moved here from California.

Will: Why would anyone move here from California?

James: Who knows! I'm just glad she did. This is the first year Alex has really liked school.

Will: *(Stops painting and looks puzzled.)* I still think it's funny that Mr. Rossi decided to retire *after* the school year began.

James: Maybe he took a look at this year's second grade class and decided to run for it! There are at least five other kids just like Alex.

Will: *(Rolling his eyes.)* Your little brother isn't *that* bad.

James: You don't live in the same house with him! Last night he put gummy worms in my bed while I was in the bathroom. I kind of shrieked when I shoved my feet down on top of them. I could hear him giggling all the way down the hall. Now every time he sees me, he squeals "Eeeeeek!" just to tease me.

Will: *(Laughing.)* Put gummy worms in *his* bed tonight.

James: No way. He'll just tell Mom and then *I'll* get in trouble. Are you almost done? I don't want to miss the buses. We're going to the mall tonight to get Alex a Halloween costume.

Will: What does he want to be?

James: I don't know, probably a pirate or some sort of bloodthirsty monster. Are you going to dress up when we take him trick-or-treating?

Will: I'm not sure yet. *(Pretends to clean off brush with rag.)*

James: I have a great troll mask! Do you want to borrow it?

Will: No, I think I have an idea. I just need to get a couple of things. *(Puts down his brush.)* I guess this is okay. Let's go!

Scene 2: Main Street Outside the School

(James and Will enter from stage right. An old mansion painted on cardboard and surrounded by caution tape serves as the background.)

James: Look! There's yellow tape around the front of the old Miller mansion!

Will: It's probably a crime scene! Who knows what goes on in that old place.

James: When we drove past it last night on the way to get pizza, Alex swore he saw a light on downstairs.

Will: Well that's just weird. No one has lived in the Miller mansion for years.

James: *(Makes spooky noises.)* I'm surprised they haven't torn it down.

Will: Yeah, I don't want it falling on me!

James: That's what the yellow tape is for—to keep people away!

Will: *(Putting up his hands.)* They don't need tape to keep me out. You couldn't pay me to go in there!

James: That place has to be haunted.

(Miss Craig enters from stage left with Emma and Kyrsten.)

Kyrsten: Good night, Miss Craig!

Miss Craig: Good night, girls! Good night, boys! Thanks for your help with the scenery, Will!

Will: The pumpkin's finished! I'll work on the spooky tree tomorrow night.

Miss Craig: I don't need the tree until Friday afternoon, so you still have a couple of days. Thanks again. Good night! *(She exits stage right.)*

James: *(Whispering.)* There aren't any cars over there. I wonder where she parked.

Emma: Maybe someone is picking her up?

James: *(Doubtfully.)* Maybe.

Emma: My mom said I can have friends over to carve pumpkins tomorrow night. Do you guys want to come?

Will: Will there be food?

Emma: *(Laughing.)* Of course there will be food, Will! Mom's making sloppy joes and nachos for everybody.

James: Sounds good!

Kyrsten: And I'm making pumpkin cupcakes with cream cheese frosting!

Will: Even better! Count me in. What time?

Emma: Come around six o'clock. And don't forget your pumpkins!

James: I might have to bring Alex with me. Is that okay?

Emma: Sure, that's fine.

Kyrsten: See you tomorrow!

James & Will: Bye!

(Girls exit stage right. Boys exit stage left.)

Scene 3: Emma's House

(The table has pumpkins, plates with snacks, and some water bottles. Emma, Kyrsten, and Will are center stage.)

Will: *(Eating a cupcake.)* These cupcakes are great!

Kyrsten: They're supposed to be for dessert, Will!

Will: I like eating dessert first!

Emma: And second and third.

Will: I *love* cupcakes.

Kyrsten: Just save some for the rest of us.

Will: You snooze; you lose! It's not my fault if you miss out.

(James and Alex enter stage right. James is carrying a bag. Alex has two small pumpkins.)

Emma: Hi, guys! I'm glad you could come!

James: Thanks for inviting us! My mom sent fruit with dip and some huge chocolate chip cookies.

Will: Mmm, cookies? Let's see! *(Takes the bag and pulls out a cookie.)*

Alex: *(Grabs the bag.)* Give me one, too!

James: *(Taking the bag back.)* You've had enough, Alex! You ate two in the car!

Alex: Do you have any gummy worms?

James: *(Rolls his eyes.)* No, Alex! They don't have gummy worms.

(Alex pouts.)

(Emma and Kyrsten talk quietly with Alex.)

James: *(Pointing to Will's costume.)* You know, Will, it isn't Halloween yet.

Will: I know that! I just decided I needed the practice putting together my costume.

James: (*Laughing.*) Well you don't see a mummy eating a cupcake and carving a pumpkin every day, that's for sure!

Will: (*Laughing.*) If I need a napkin, I'm all set!

James: Guess what I saw on the way over?

Will: (*Munching on a cookie.*) I don't know. What?

James: There were lights on in the old Miller mansion again!

(*Emma moves over next to James.*)

Emma: Did you see them, too? My mom said there were lights on when she went past on her way home from work.

Kyrsten: That's really creepy. It's been empty for as long as I can remember. Maybe it really *is* haunted!

Emma: Anyone want to go exploring tonight?

Will: Not me! I was invited to carve pumpkins and eat. That's what I came for.

Kyrsten: I really don't want to see any ghosts, Emma!

James: I'll go!

Alex: Me, too!

James: *(Shaking his head.)* You can't go. You're too little.

Emma: I think it would be cool if the Miller mansion is haunted! That house is over 200 years old. I bet some amazing things have happened there.

James: *(Rubbing his hands together.)* And October's a good time for ghost hunting. It's only three more days until Halloween.

Will: *(Sits down and folds his arms over his chest.)* I don't want any part of this!

Kyrsten: Me, either!

Emma: I guess we'd better just carve our pumpkins tonight, James.

James: *(Whispering.)* But maybe we could take a look at the mansion when I take Alex trick-or-treating Friday night! Will and I were going to dress up anyway.

Emma: *(Whispering back.)* Kyrsten and I are, too! That's a great idea. I'll talk to you about it later!

Scene 4: Halloween Night

(Turn the lights out. Emma, Will, and Kyrsten walk down the center aisle toward the stage. They are carrying flashlights and trick-or-treating bags.)

Will: It's windy tonight.

Kyrsten: And cold, too. It's kind of spooky out here with all the bare trees.

Emma: And look, Kyrsten! The moon is full! *(Howling.) Owwwoooo!*

Kyrsten: Stop that!

Alex: *(Walks on from stage right. James is following him. Both are wearing their costumes.)* Thanks for the popcorn! *(Alex waves to someone offstage.)*

James: You have a ton of candy. Are you ready to quit?

Alex: No way! I'm just getting started.

Emma: Look, James! Do you see what I see?

(Stage crew shines a light from stage left.)

James: *Cool!* There's a light in the Miller mansion tonight!

Will: Okay, I'm done if you guys are planning to go down there.

Emma: James and I thought we'd just walk by it. And maybe peek in the windows.

Kyrsten: Then I'm going home!

Emma: You can't walk home alone, Kyrsten. All we want to do is have a look around. I promise we won't go in.

Kyrsten: I'm staying right here on the sidewalk with Will. You and James can look around.

Emma: *(Rolls her eyes.)* Fine with me!

Alex: *(Spins around in his costume and sings.)* I love candy! I love candy!

James: *(Grabs Alex.)* Okay, you're cut off.

Alex: I only ate ten candy bars!

James: *(Slaps his hand to his forehead.)* Oh, Alex! Mom will never let me take you trick-or-treating again! You're supposed to wait until we get home to eat anything. Stay here with Will and Kyrsten. Emma and I will be right back.

Alex: I want to see the ghost! I'm coming with you.

Emma: No, you're not, Alex.

Alex: I am! I am! I am! (*Runs toward the Miller mansion and then falls down.*) Owww! (*Alex starts to cry.*)

James: (*Running after Alex.*) Oh man, now he got hurt!

(*Turn stage or room lights on.*)

Kyrsten: The porch light just came on!

Will: I'd better go help.

Kyrsten: I'll go too! I'm not staying here alone!

Will: The door is opening! Do something!

Kyrsten: What do you want me to do?

James: *(Kneeling down by Alex.)* Come on, Alex! Let's get out of here!

(Miss Craig enters stage left.)

Emma: Wait! Is that . . . ?

Kyrsten: Miss Craig?

Miss Craig: Alex, are you okay?

Alex: I hurt my knee!

James: I don't understand. What are you doing here, Miss Craig?

Miss Craig: *(Laughing.)* I live here! This was my grandfather's house.

James: So you've been turning the lights on at night?

Miss Craig: Well, it *is* hard to see at night without any lights. Why don't you all come inside and I'll explain. I need to find a Band-Aid for Alex's knee. You can have some cookies and hot chocolate.

Emma, Kyrsten, Will, & **James:** *(Looking at each other.)* Sure!

Scene 5: The Mansion

(Everyone is onstage. There is a table with mugs and cookies.)

Emma: So, you moved here from California because your grandfather died?

Miss Craig: Yes, he had been in a nursing home for a long time.

Kyrsten: None of us ever remember anyone living here. It's always been empty.

Miss Craig: Well, I always loved this house. I used to visit it when I was a little girl. Then last year when my grandfather died, he left it to me in his will.

Will: It's a big house for one person.

Miss Craig: It is a big house, but I really want to fix it up. There's a lot to do. I hired Emma's dad to be my contractor.

Emma: I didn't know that!

James: So that's why the yellow tape was up on Tuesday.

Miss Craig: Yes, they're putting in a new sidewalk. I think that's why Alex tripped. I hadn't turned on my porch light because the front yard isn't safe for trick-or-treating.

James: Well, Alex is kind of a klutz. *And* he's had way too much sugar tonight.

Alex: *(Jumping up and down.)* Do you have any gummy worms?

Miss Craig: No, Alex. I'm sorry, I don't!

Alex: Can I have another cookie?

James: No!

(Alex crawls under the table.)

Miss Craig: Why did all of you look so startled when I opened the door?

Kyrsten: We thought your house was haunted.

Miss Craig: Well, if it is, they must be very happy ghosts! This house was always filled with laughter when I was little. I have such good memories of spending my summers here.

Emma: Well, so much for ghost hunting!

James: Yeah, there's always next year. I really wanted to see a ghost!

Alex: *(Crawls out from under the table with the tablecloth over his head.)* Ooooooo!

The End

Adapting Readers' Theater Scripts

Readers' theater can be done very simply. Performers just read their lines from scripts. They don't have to memorize them! And, they don't have to move around. The performers sit on chairs or stools while reading their parts.

Adapted Readers' Theater: This looks more like a regular play. The performers wear makeup and costumes. The stage has scenery and props. The cast moves around to show the action. Performers can still read from their scripts.

A Puppet Show: Some schools and libraries have puppet collections. Or students can create puppets. Students make the puppets be the actors. They read their scripts for their puppets.

Teaching Guides

Readers' Theater Teaching Guides are available online at **abdopublishing.com**. Each guide includes printable scripts, reading levels for each character, and additional production tips for each play. Get yours today!

Websites

To learn more about Readers' Theater, visit **booklinks.abdopublishing.com**. These links are routinely monitored and updated to provide the most current information available.

FEB   2016   2 1982 02907 5888